BUTTERFLIES

Trevor Terry &
Margaret Linton

Illustrated by
Jackie Harland

Language Consultant:
Diana Bentley
University of Reading

Puffin Books

Contents

All the words that are
in **bold** are explained in
the glossary on page 31.

Beautiful swallowtail butterflies.

Butterflies are beautiful **insects**. The swallowtail butterfly is one of the most beautiful. In some countries there are lots of swallowtails. In other countries, like Britain, there are very few. These swallowtail butterflies are living in a marshy place.

The butterflies feed from flowers.

Swallowtails, like most butterflies, live for only a short time. On sunny days they fly around looking for food. They feed on a sweet juice called **nectar**. Nectar is found in flowers. In the picture, the female butterfly is sucking up nectar.

Swallowtails mate in early summer.

The male butterfly is smaller than the female. In early summer, male butterflies look for females. They fly above the marsh together. Then they settle on a plant to **mate**. After mating, the females are ready to lay their eggs.

A swallowtail lays her eggs.

The eggs must be laid on the right kind of plant. A female often chooses a plant called milk parsley. She flies to different leaves and lays one egg at a time. The eggs are greenish-yellow.

The eggs hatch into caterpillars.

The eggs change to a pale pinkish-brown colour. After about a week they **hatch**. From each egg comes a tiny **caterpillar**. The swallowtail caterpillar is black, with a white patch in the middle of its body.

The caterpillars feed and grow.

The caterpillar has strong jaws. It eats lots of milk parsley leaves and grows quickly. It grows too big for its skin. The old skin drops off and a new skin grows. This is called **moulting**. The caterpillar rests while its new skin hardens.

The beautiful swallowtail caterpillar.

After about a month the caterpillar is fully grown. It has moulted four times. Now it is green. It has black stripes with orange spots. The caterpillar's back legs help it to move and to hold on to the leaves.

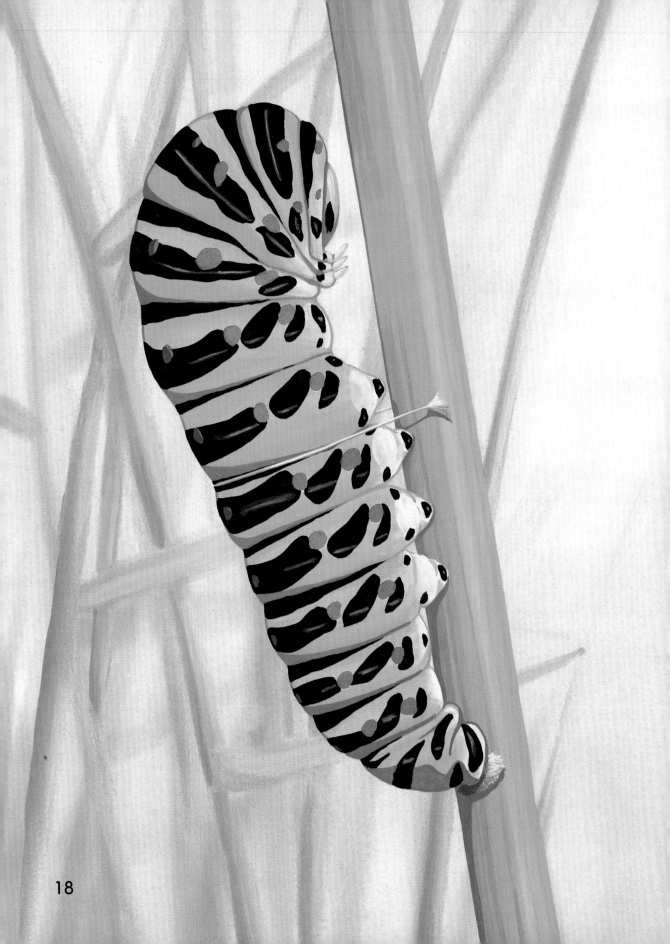

The caterpillar begins to rest.

Soon the caterpillar will change again.
But first, it needs to find somewhere to
rest. It often chooses the stem of a tall
reed plant. The caterpillar fastens itself
to the reed by spinning a silk pad and a
silk loop.

The caterpillar turns into a chrysalis.

After a few days, the caterpillar's skin begins to split. Inside is a new creature. It is called a **chrysalis**. The chrysalis looks very different from the caterpillar. At first its skin is soft, but later it becomes hard.

The chrysalis rests during the winter.

The chrysalis may be yellowish-green or brown. It is still held on to the reed stem by the silk loop and pad. The chrysalis does not eat, and it sleeps all winter. Inside, it slowly changes into a butterfly.

A swallowtail butterfly comes out of the chrysalis.

In spring, as the weather gets warmer, the chrysalis begins to wake up. The skin splits right along its back. Slowly the swallowtail butterfly starts to crawl out. The chrysalis case is left behind on the reed stem.

The swallowtail butterfly is ready to fly away.

The butterfly hangs on to the reed stem. Its wings are crumpled and damp. It cannot fly yet. Soon its wings become stronger. They flatten and spread out. Then they become dry. The young swallowtail is ready to fly away.

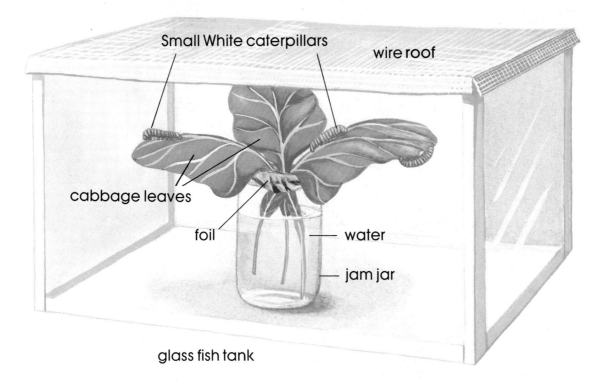

Small White caterpillars

wire roof

cabbage leaves

foil

water

jam jar

glass fish tank

Keeping caterpillars.

Caterpillars can be kept in a fish tank, like the one in the picture. Always feed the caterpillars on the leaves of the plant on which they were found. Make sure you change the leaves often. Keep the inside of the cage clean.

△ Small Tortoiseshell caterpillars feed on stinging nettles.

△ Small White caterpillars feed on cabbage leaves.

△ Painted Lady caterpillars feed on thistles.

The life cycle of a butterfly.

How many stages of the life cycle can you remember?

Glossary

Caterpillar The grub (or larva) of a butterfly which hatches from an egg.

Chrysalis A resting stage when a caterpillar changes into a butterfly.

Hatch To break out of an egg.

Insects Small animals without a backbone. They have three pairs of legs, and usually two pairs of wings. Their bodies are covered by a hard skin.

Mate This is when male (father) and female (mother) animals join together. It is how a baby animal is started.

Moulting This is when the caterpillar (or larva) gets rid of its skin. The caterpillar has grown too big for it. It needs a new skin so that it can go on growing.

Nectar A sweet juice found in flowers. Some insects, like butterflies, feed on it. Bees use it for making honey.

Finding out more

Here are some books to read to find out more about butterflies.

Butterflies by A. Watson (Kingfisher Books, 1981)
Butterflies and Moths by H. Pluckrose (Hamish Hamilton, 1980)
Butterfly Watching by P. E. S. Whalley (Severn House, 1980)
Caterpillars and Moths by A. Braithwaite (Dinosaur, 1983)
Discovering Butterflies and Moths by K. Porter (Wayland, 1986)

Index